★ ★ ★ ★ ★ ★ ★ ★ ★ ★ ★ ★ ★ ★ ★ ★ ★ ★ ★

NO NATURAL BORN
LEADERS

★ ★ ★ ★ ★ ★ ★ ★ ★ ★ ★ ★ ★ ★ ★ ★ ★ ★ ★

★★★★★★★★★★★★★★★★★★★★★★★★★★★★★★★★★★★

NO NATURAL BORN
LEADERS

A Study in the Art of Leadership

★★★★★★★★★★★★★★★★★★★★★★★★★★★★★★★★★★★

by:
BOB DANMYER

authorHOUSE®

AuthorHouse™
1663 Liberty Drive
Bloomington, IN 47403
www.authorhouse.com
Phone: 1-800-839-8640

Published by AuthorHouse   06/20/2012

ISBN: 978-1-4685-4608-8 (sc)
ISBN: 978-1-4685-4607-1 (hc)
ISBN: 978-1-4685-4606-4 (e)

Library of Congress Control Number: 2012901290

Special thanks to Keith, Lance, Lenny and Leslie

ABOUT THE AUTHOR

BOB DANMYER

Born in Baltimore, Maryland in 1941, he attended high school at Baltimore City College, graduating in 1959. Bob has also obtained an AA degree in Business and a BA in Human Relations, and is a graduate of the United States Army Command and General Staff College. He secured his first management position in 1967 at Maryland Cup Corporation. Well known by the brand name, Sweetheart Products, Maryland Cup Corporation was sold in 1982. However, the brand name Sweetheart Products has survived. Maryland Cup was a fortune five hundred company and at one time the largest manufacturer of paper cups in the world. During his time at Maryland Cup he managed three separated departments and had a total of nine supervisors that reported directly to him. He was instrumental in the Corporation being awarded many awards for their achievements in narrow web flexographic printing from the "Flexographic Technical Association". The departments that he managed for many years lead the Owings Mills, Maryland Plant in the number of monthly Plant Managers Awards for Excellence.

While working at Maryland Cup in 1965 he joined the Maryland National Guard's 20th Special Forces (Green Berets).

He served in Special Forces for fourteen years working his way up from Private to Captain. After transferring from the Special Forces, due to injuries he sustained from a serious military parachuting accident, he continued his part time military service serving in several other Guard units.

In 1985 he went to work full-time in the National Guard system where he served on the Adjutant General of Maryland's staff for a total of seventeen years, as both a Military Technician and State of Maryland government employee. Bob Danmyer was also an instructor during his full and part time military career at the Maryland Military Academy and taught leadership to future military leaders.

Bob Danmyer holds numerous military decorations the highest of which is the Army's Legion of Merit and two State of Maryland Distinguished Service Crosses, the latter being the highest awards given by the State of Maryland. He retired from the military in 2001 at the rank of Brevet Colonel with thirty-six years of service.

After his military service he went to work for the Maryland Military Department as the Program Director of the "About Face", drug demand reduction program. When the program was discontinued in 2003, Bob left the Military Department and went to work for the Department of Army as a Department of Defense (DOD) contractor at Fort Detrick, Maryland. He was put in charge of the armed security force charge with maintaining the security and safety of the almost 8000 people that lived and worked at the facility.

With a total forty-five years of leadership and management experience, Bob Danmyer retired in 2008, and lives with his wife Leslie in Hanover, Pennsylvania. Today he writes, travels, plays golf, is an avid hunter and also enjoys radio-controlled model aviation.

CHAPTERS

INTRODUCTION

Leadership, the word alone inspires thoughts of Caesar, Richard the Lion Hearted, Washington, Churchill, Eisenhower, Kennedy and Reagan. Where and how did they learn leadership? Think about this, they all had military backgrounds. Of the world's great learning institutions I question how many have even attempted to teach leadership. The military teaches leadership at almost every level to those who will lead their soldiers, sailors and airmen; how many corporations do the same? More over, when have you seen a university class schedule that offered a course called Leadership 101, or Senior Leadership? A course entitled Introduction to Management is not about leadership. The words leader and manager have two very different meanings.

Some people like to think that leaders are born, that the craft comes naturally, that they need no training. While it is true that some personalities are more suited to the leadership role, without training so called natural born leaders sometimes make the worst leaders. Diamonds have to be polished in order to shine!

How about the world's great corporate institutions, surely they are teaching leadership. If so are they doing it at the lowest level? Where does the mechanic who gets promoted to shop foreman and suddenly put in charge get leadership training? Also, I believe with the number of people serving in the military decreasing, there is a dangerous shortage of good leaders and a growing number of bad ones. If you do not believe this, talk to your friends and family members about their immediate boss, or their company. Ask how they are being treated as workers and more importantly human beings? The answers you will hear are the primary reasons I am writing this book.

As a former leadership instructor and supervisor in the military, the government and the corporate world I can no longer be silent! Today more then ever this great country needs great leaders to rise to the occasion and keep America strong. Where is the next Washington or Kennedy? While this book will not instantly make you a great leader, it will improve your leadership skills, and challenge your mind to learn more about this important subject.

CHAPTER 1

What Happened To America?

Many people look around the Untied States today and ask, "What Happened to America?" are we losing our greatness? How did we arrive at our current state? Why does it cost so much to live in this great nation? Where are all the jobs? I hear people say, "I don't understand how this all happened". Why is it that the Japanese and Chinese have out-paced us in the world market place? It should be so apparent, but our nations leaders have just recently found the vision to accurately define the cause of these problems. Maybe I can shed some light on what is at the core of our current dilemma. We live in a modern, mobile society, with a thirst for fuel like no other nation on earth. We like to be warm in the winter and cool in the summer. We are spoiled. But, the cost of energy is ten times higher today than it was fifty years ago and every adult American owns one or two cars, and I am not talking only about the wealthy. We have to live in a house with four bedrooms and it must be at least three thousand square feet in size. Because of these two key points, this nation uses 25% of the world's crude oil! Because Americans are large people we love large cars, but now we call them SUV's (Sport Utility Vehicles). Most Americans are just physically too big for small cars; therefore we are slow to be drawn to them. Greed has caused American businesses to spend the last thirty years sending all of our manufacturing jobs overseas. You cannot pick up a piece of clothing today that is made in America. Also, American employers have forgotten how to treat their most valuable resource, their employees. What has happened to the signs that used to hang over the factory gates that said, "Through these gates walk the finest people in the world our employees"? To Big Business I would ask, do you think that if American jobs go overseas because of cheap labor, Americans will have money to buy your products?

The sad part of all this is that after World War II America owned the World market place! We basically bombed all of our competitors out of business during the big war. American factories that made the tools of war quickly converted to the production of airliners, modern electronic products for the home, automobiles and numerous other items to create a comfortable life for all that had survived the horror of war. As fast as America produced the World was waiting to buy. We could not make our products fast enough! We told workers that the more they produced, the more money they would be paid, and it was called piecework. Quality was secondary to quantity! I can remember when a car was only built to last three years. Tires were only good for fifteen to twenty thousand miles. The Japanese made us pay dearly for this mistake! Remember when everything made in Japan was referred to as Jap Crap. When the words, Made in the USA meant quality! For a variety of reasons those words are starting to mean that again. One of the reasons for this change is that most products made today in foreign countries break shortly after they are purchased. Cheap does not mean better, you get what you pay for. Many people believe that some foreign manufacturers built planned failure into all of their products, which creates a continuing need for replacement. I own an old clothes iron that was made in America, maybe thirty years ago. I bought it to wax my snow skies, and it has been used a great deal in the last twenty-five years, and it still works. In the same time period, I have replaced a total of nine clothes irons that were made in the Far East. In all of the replacement situations it would have costs more to get the broken one fixed then the product was worth, so I just went out and bought a new iron. While I was buying all of these irons made mostly in China, I drove their economy uphill while ours was going down. You may think this is fabricated, but as I am writing this chapter the remote mouse that I bought last year for my computer keeps falling apart. Guess where it was made? China. However, our elected leaders just don't get it and we continue to trade with the Chinese instead of making it better in America.

In the sixties and seventies America lost their dominance in the world markets because we read markets wrong and many of our products were not high quality. Fortunately, that did change and today America has its' quality act together, but at what cost? I predict that the Chinese will lose their markets for the same reasons we did in the past, poor quality. Unfortunately, today when you go to the store to buy something, say an electrical component, everything in the store is made in China, and there are no buying options.

The Chinese make cars, but the quality is too poor to sell them in this country; I am sure that will change. In China one of the best selling cars is General Motors Buick and it is because the Chinese believe it is a quality product. We could sell more if China would let us bring more into the country. What happened to fair trade? All of these things have happened because of bad leadership, bad leadership decisions, and a complete lack of long-range vision and, yes, a little greed.

In this book I will go back to basics, and discuss things that are just not taught in MBA (Masters in Business Administration) courses. We must start out by understanding the defined difference in a manager and a leader. Managers manage resources, leaders lead people. A manager controls and directs, a leader shows the way for people to follow. A leader unlocks the power of collective thinking by using the brainpower of everyone that works for him or her, down to the lowest levels. A manager makes all the decisions in order to control and because they trust no one, they are glaring examples of the "One Smart Person" management methodology. By the way, most people who work for such an individual are miserable, because they have no input into the process! Guess those managers were never taught what my grandmother used to say; "Three heads are better then one". Remember today a good CEO (Chief Executive Officer) or supervisor must be more than just a manager; they must also be a good leader.

In the following chapters, I will proceed to discuss what it takes to be a good leader. Together, we will look at the tools that will allow you to develop and improve your leadership skills. Read and learn how to be a born leader!

CHAPTER 2

The Great One

W. Edwards Deming

The gentleman I am going to tell you about and his management philosophy has filled books, not just a short chapter. Today in America if you would ask most people in business if they know the name, W. Edwards Deming they might just look at you with a puzzled stare. Ask that same question in Japan and you might get a detailed explanation lasting several minutes. The really sad part of Doctor Deming's life is that just when his management methodology was starting to take hold in America he passed away at the age of ninety-three. It is funny, that after years of studying and teaching Deming, I can tell you that I remember exactly where I was when he died on December 20, 1993. I was eating dinner in a small restaurant off the town square in Santa Fe, New Mexico. I can testify, as the Star War fans say, I felt a change in the Force.

W. Edwards Deming was born in 1900, in Sioux City, Iowa and raised in Polk, Iowa. The son of well-educated parents, his father had studied mathematics and law, his mother music in San Francisco. Deming was married twice surviving both of his wives. He obtained degrees in electrical engineering from the University of Wyoming, a Masters from the University of Colorado, and in 1928 a PHD from Yale. Both of the upper level degrees were in the discipline that he loved most, mathematics. Doctor Deming also studied at the University College in London, England in 1936.

In the late twenties Doctor Deming was introduced to Walter A. Shewhart who worked for Bell Laboratories. Inspired by Shewhart's work in statistical process control he wrote and had a book published in 1939, called Statistical Methods from the Viewpoint of Quality Control. In fact Deming copied many of Shewhart's techniques and methods of statistical process control.

During World War II, Doctor Deming's quality control methods were incorporated into the production of material being produced for the war effort. Deming also taught statistical process control methods to the workers of the Arsenal of Democracy. When the war was over, because of the demand for American products overseas, as discussed in chapter one, his quality control methods stopped being used. The emphasis came off quality and on quantity. Remember, we dominated the world market place and we could afford to shift to this mindset. In the mid-forties Deming continued trying to educate American manufacturing on the benefits of his methodology but with no success.

Because of work he had done for the United States Census Bureau in the early forties, Doctor Deming was asked by the America Army of Occupation in 1947 to come to Japan and help with the census. At the time Japanese industry was a disaster! Also, before World War II the Japanese were not known for making quality products. With most of their factories covered in rubble the Japanese started to rebuild their manufacturing processes in a unique and innovative way. They would install a large drive motor at the end of a city block. It was in turn connected to a long drive shaft that ran the entire length of that block. The individual businesses in the area would hook up to the shaft through drive belts. The drive motor would then start-up and stop at scheduled times everyday, usually at the beginning and end of the workday. Each business on the block used the power from the shaft to drive the machinery that manufactured their specific products. In 1996 I spent some time in Japan, and I can tell you that this is a far cry from the way Japanese industry works today. As a child in the later forties and early fifties my parents gave me toys, made in Japan, that if you took them apart they were made out of Budweiser beer cans. The words Made in Japan meant very low quality!

While in Japan Deming became involved with Japanese society and this eventually lead to his association with the

Japanese Union of Scientist and Engineers (JUSE). Members of JUSE had in the past studied Shewhart's methods of statistical process control. In Japan there is a saying, "That when the student is ready the teacher will come". With the coming of Deming, and the condition of Japan's industry, never was this statement more accurate. JUSE enlisted Deming to teach his methods to key leaders of Japanese industry. The primary message and theme of Deming's training was, improved quality reduces expense while increasing productivity and market share. In other words, quality products will eventually capture their markets. One only has to look at the Japanese auto industry as a glaring example of the success of this philosophy. In 1950 JUSE, as a way of honoring Deming for all of his work, established and awarded for the first time the Deming Prize. The award is still presented in Japan to companies that have excelled in the pursuit of quality. Japan in 1960 bestowed one of the highest honors the country has on Deming, the Order of Sacred Treasures, Second Class, for breathing life back into the nations industry.

Upon returning to the United States Deming began his own consulting business. He was featured in a National Broadcasting documentary in 1980 called "If Japan can, why can't we?" This national exposure greatly increased the demand for his services. A Ford executive that had seen the National Broadcasting documentary on Deming brought him to the attention of the company's management team. In 1981 Ford's share of the automotive market place was dropping. The company was in grave danger of going out of business. As a result, Doctor Deming was recruited by the newly appointed Division Quality Manager, John A. Manoogian, to start a quality movement at Ford. Deming immediately determined that the culture at Ford was not on track and that upper management was creating the majority of the problems. With Demings help Ford changed the direction of the company away from low quality, fuel guzzling large cars to smaller high quality, fuel-efficient vehicles. By 1986 Ford's profits started soaring, and for the first time since the 1920's exceeded the profits of their American competitors, General Motors and Chrysler. From this point on the demand for Deming services also soared with dozens of American companies seeking his services. This was the beginning of the Quality Revolution in America.

When you look at the Deming philosophy, you see that it is designed around fourteen key management points. Deming believed that management, not unions or employees create the culture of a business. If you are going to change a work culture you must start at the top. There is a story that Deming, who was known for his direct approach to issues, had been hired to train a group of key corporate executives. The Chief Executive Officer (CEO) introduced Deming and then proceeded to leave. As he turned around he saw that Deming was walking out with him. The story goes that he stopped and said to Deming, "Why are you leaving?" we hired you to speak and teach at this gathering. Deming replied that if the CEO was leaving so was he! That without the CEO present showing his commitment to the process of change, anything that Deming did or said would be a waste of time; the CEO stayed for the entire session. Deming taught that change and commitment to a process must always start at the top.

Once again remember at the center of the Deming philosophy are fourteen points of light. Let us take a brief look at all fourteen:

1. **Constancy of Purpose**
   - Continuously improve to be competitive, and stay in business and provide jobs. <u>Everyday</u> think of ways to make products and processes better.
   - Plan for tomorrow; don't just focus on today's problems. Senior leaders should at a minimum have a five-year plan. When employee's work for an organization invested in the future, they feel secure.

2. **Adopt the New "Deming" Philosophy**
   - Awaken to the challenge, management must learn their responsibilities and take on leadership for a change. Note: Remember management owns the system, not the workers!
   - Develop a new religion that will not accept poor quality services and products.
   - Higher quality cost less, not more!
   - Productivity increases as quality improves—why? Less rework!
   - Focus on the process rather than profit, on the team rather than the individual, on the customer rather than the stockholder.

3. **Cease Dependency on Inspections**
   - Build quality into the product from the beginning.

- Prevent the occurrence of defects by improving the process and listening to customers before producing the product.
- Companies typically pay workers to make defects then correct them. This is very costly!

4. **Require Suppliers to Provide Statistical Evidence of Quality.**
   - Reduce that number of suppliers for the same item by eliminating those not having statistical evidence of quality.
   - End the practice of awarding business solely on the basis of price. Note: Remember you generally get what you pay for! Giving contracts to the lowest bidder often leads to low quality parts and supplies. Dr. Deming stated: "Price has no meaning without the measure of the quality being purchased."

5. **Improve Constantly and Forever**
   - When you constantly improve quality and productivity, you constantly cut cost.

   Note: *The old theory that states, "If it is not broken don't mess with it", does not work. <u>Always improve the product or process!</u>*

6. **Train All Employees**
   - Companies should institute on the job training at all levels, top to bottom. Training is a major investment in your employees and the future of the business. However,

when budgets get cut training is usually the first thing to be reduced or eliminated.

7. **Institute Modern Methods of Supervision**
    - A supervisor today must be more than a judge or an overseer; they must be a manager, leader, coach and teacher.
    - The primary job of the supervisor must be to develop their people so they can continually improve and do a better job.

Note: *Once again, let me repeat, management is generally responsible for most of the problems not the workers! Why, because management controls the system, and employees work within the system. If things are not working, look at fixing the system, not fixing the blame on employees!*

8. **Encourage Free Communications—Drive Out Fear!**
    - Workers who do not understand their job and who are afraid to ask questions will continue to do things wrong. This can be dangerous!
    - Employees that fear their supervisors may be afraid to point out problems or defective processes, fearing blame or retaliation.

Note: *These two points cost business millions of dollars every year, and in some cases lives. Unlock the collective thinking power of your employees! Practice management by walking around and asking questions! If you really want to solve problems talk to the employees, seek their input.*

9. **Breakdown Barriers Between Departments**
   - Promote teamwork . . . Eliminate "We vs. Them" Environments
   - Remove the walls between offices and department!
   - Do away with separate dining rooms for management and workers!
   - Locate operations in the same buildings encouraging the team concept.
   - Engineering should not be on one side of town and production on the other.
   - Engineers and production workers should work side by side.
   - Think TEAMWORK!

10. **Eliminate Poster and Slogans**
    - Poster and slogans only generate frustration and resentment among workers if management fails to provide the means to the end the slogan proclaims.
    - Slogans often suggest that workers can do better if they only try harder.
    - There is no substitute for training, knowledge of the process and for the tools and methods to do the job.

11. **Eliminate Work Standards**
    - Quotas lead to frustration, chaos, and employee turnover. Not everyone can work at the same speed and create quality products or services.
    - Once workers have completed their quotas, they quit working and linger around until the end of the workday.

- A sure fire way of getting defective products is to pay for piecework.

Note: *Deming developed an exercise that he used at all of his training seminars; it was called the "Red Bead Exercise". I recommend that you go to UTUBE and type in "Deming Red Bead Exercise"; this video will be very helpful in understanding Deming's eleventh point.*

12. Remove Barriers to Pride in Workmanship

- People want to do a good job!
- Misguided supervisors, faulty equipment and defective material stand in the way.
- These barriers must be removed

13. Institute a Vigorous Program of Education and Self-Improvement

- Keep personnel apace with changes in materials, method, product design and technology.
- Education and training prepare people for new jobs.
- Education and training provide new skills to utilize new technology.
- Management must recognize that educating and training their workers is an investment and not an expense.

14. Create a Structure in Top Management that Pushes Everyday on the Above 14 Points.

Everyone in an organization must be dedicated to making the transformation to quality. James G. Belcher, in his book "Productivity Plus" said it best, "Establishing a productivity change process is a change effort and never comes easy. You cannot mandate change and you cannot delegate responsibility for change. Attitude and behaviors are to ingrained and organizational systems to entrenched. Senior management must not only raise the banner, but must also lead the charge."

Deming also identified what he referred to as the "Seven Deadly Diseases" which can destroy organizations, they are:

1. Lack of constancy of purpose
2. Emphasis on short-term profits
3. Evaluation by performance, merit rating or annual review
4. Mobility of management
5. Running a company on visible figures alone.
6. Excessive medical cost
7. Excessive cost of warranty, fueled by lawyers who work for contingency fees.

It is my opinion that the core of the Deming philosophy rests in two key issues. First, do not shoot from the hip and make business decision based on a personal opinion or best guess. Make important decisions based on statistical data; Deming used to say, "In God we trust, and all others can bring data". Second, empower your work force and your customers; doing this unlocks the collective think power of an organization. It may take longer to get a solution to a problem, but it will be the best solution. Many supervisors think that if they empower their people this means giving up control. You must remember that the leader is always the final decision maker, and responsible for the final outcome. You can delegate power but not responsibility! When the Deming system is instituted into an organization the benefits are: problems get solved permanently, the quality of work life is improved, everyone is able to work better and communication and coordination improves. To learn more about W. Edwards Deming and his system of management, I recommend reading one of his primary literary works, "Out of Crisis". It is worth the time to learn more about this major force in business, in both the 20th and 21st centuries.

CHAPTER 3

Levels Of Leadership

This chapter will cover how organizations and working staffs should be organized, for any organization to be successful. I have seen many operations where a supervisor or business owner is taking years off their lives, and leading the organization to failure for two simple reasons. First, because they trust no one or they think they are the smartest person in the organization, they will not ask for employee input, nor will they delegate. Second, they have done no long range planning, and have no vision of the future for their organization! They are running the business in my opinion on a wing and a prayer; time will catch up with them if a heart attack does not first.

This will be the point in this chapter where I revert a great deal to my military training and background. There is a sound reason for this. Some of you may not be aware of this fact, but the earliest example of an organized institution was the Roman Army. If you study the history of the Roman Army you will find that they fought an organized battle, which resulted in the defeat of many forces superior in numbers. Roman military tactics and organization is still studied today in all major military schools. All great military leaders are students of history. Anyone who has served at the leadership level in the military clearly understands that a well-organized unit will generally be successful. However, you cannot do it all on your own, you need help. As your organization grows this will be even more apparent, you need a staff!

Military staffs are organized as follows: S1 Personnel/ Administration, S2 Intelligence, S3 Operations and Training, S4 Logistics/Supply and S5 Civil Affairs/ Psychological Operations. It is very easy to translate this staffing matrix into civilian business language by stating the positions this way, S1 Personnel/ Administration, S2 Marketing and Sales, S3 Operations/Training, S4 Logistics/Supply and S5 Public Affairs. Can you see the parallels I just made? I believe it is not necessary to detail out where areas of responsibility fall under each staff area. The staff title alone defines those areas where the various organizational tasks should be delegated, once you apply common sense. Remember that you can and should delegate your authority to staff members, but you can never delegate your responsibility. The staff should meet at a minimum, once a week for purposes of coordination and communication.

Now let us address the levels of leadership. The military is organized into three levels: strategic, operational and tactical. I will relate them to business by saying that a business structure should be organized in three levels, senior management, middle management and lower level management. It is not hard if you are working in management for an organization to figure out at which level you find yourself. However, it is critical that you understand the responsibly leaders have at the different levels. Let's start by looking at these three key levels! In doing so I will start at the lowest level and work up to the highest, which is the most important of the three levels. Lower level supervisors are positioned inside an organization where the rubber meets the road. They are called by titles such as "lead mechanic", "shop foreman" or "yard boss". They are working leaders that get into the dirt right beside people. They must be technically proficient in the day-to-day operations of the element they supervise. Lower level leaders are the ones that actually turn the directives and vision of upper level management into reality. Their planning cycle is never longer than a few months in length. Much of what they do requires them to be reactive, quick thinkers, and good with people. If they are not the latter the entire unit is unhappy and non-productive. They can raise or lower the workers perspective of the organization. Company image is in their hands much more than the supervisors at the middle and upper levels of an organization. These supervisors are generally chosen because they are the most technically proficient, have been on the job the longest, or have the most education. All of these reasons for making a selection may not be the best. In many cases they may know the most, but are not good with people, are poor organizers, cannot work under stress and are not reliable. To add insult to injury we further set them up for failure by not providing them with some leadership and management training. When I looked at an individual for this type of position, I would usually look for someone with a solid leadership background. Which in may cases they have received in the military, by playing organized sports or being a leaders in academic clubs and projects. Also, when I say they must be good with people, that does not mean they have to be the most popular individual in the shop; leadership is not a popularity contest. However, they must be fair and just, showing no favoritism. People can learn the technical side of an operation much easier then character and personality. Above all, such leaders must be loyal to their people and loyal to the orders and management directives they receive from their superiors.

Mid-level supervision, in my opinion, is the most stressful level! Why, because they are positioned between management and lower level supervisors. They must possess the intellectual capacity to communicate both up and down the chain of command. Their planning cycle is usually one to two years out. The sad reality today is the selection of most middle managers is based on years of education as opposed to years of experience and a proven track record of success. Some of the best middle managers I have seen only had a high school education. They started at the bottom, were smart, great with people, had outstanding organizational skills; task oriented and because of all of this had been successful at everything they did. But, the most important character trait they possessed was they were outstanding communicators. They had the ability to convey orders and directives in a clear and concise manner. Moreover people were not afraid to bring things to their attention. I have known commanders that if the unit was running out of ammunition during an attack no one would tell them, because they were afraid of how they would react. A key point to mention is that I would never put someone in charge at any level with a dictatorial style of leadership; this will come back to haunt you!

An excellent example of how a dictatorial style of leadership can lead to the failure of an organization is found in the Allied

Invasion of Europe on June 6, 1944, known as D-Day. Erwin Rommel, known as the Desert Fox, Adolph Hitler's greatest general's was in charge of the defense of Northern France, specifically the invasion site, Normandy Beach.

Erwin Johannes Eugen Rommel

Generalfeldmarschall Erwin Rommel

Rommel always believed that when the Allied Invasion came the first twenty-four hours would be decisive. The day of the invasion, Rommel was in Germany celebrating his wife's birthday. When informed that the invasion had begun he requested permission to use forces being held in reserve close to the invasion site. This force had a high concentration of armor and could have easily defeated the light infantry forces landing on the beach. The force in question was under the direct control of Rommel's Commander and Chief, and the leader of the German people, Adolph Hitler. Hitler was well known for going into rants when given bad news. The evening before the invasion he had taken a sedative and gone to bed. His staff knowing his mood was afraid to wake him to get the needed permission. Rommel, one of the greatest military minds of his time, said that when the Allied invasion of Europe started it must be defeated on the beach. The rest is history, the reserves were released too late and the Allies secured a foothold at Normandy. One year later Hitler was dead and Nazi Germany defeated. I wonder how empowered General Rommel felt on that fateful day in 1944. History has shown that dictators, like Hitler generally wind-up assassinated! That statement may be realistic for history and politics, but people generally do not physically attack their boss. However, dictatorial supervisors get assassinated in a different way. Their employees withhold important information from them, and they plot for their removal in ways you cannot imagine. Dictatorial supervisors in many cases are one of the primary reasons for companies going union. Think about my example of dictatorial styles of leadership when selecting supervisors.

George Smith Patton, Jr.

Now let me address the most important level of supervision, the Senior Level. Lieutenant General George S. Patton, one of the greatest military leaders of World War II once said, "Wars may be fought by weapons, but are won by men. It is the spirit of the men who follows the man who leads that gains victory". In business success depends on well-motivated men and women, who are led by competent leaders. An organization will be ineffective unless it has a senior leader that can motivate and direct subordinate staffs and provide them with a purpose and vision to succeed. Two of the keys to success at the Senior Leadership level are to "Keep your people informed" and "Insure that a task is understood, supervised and accomplished". These two things are the greatest challenges that a senior leader faces. You must communicate these things in a way that everyone understands at every level. Napoleon, the great French military mind of the 19th century had a low ranking soldier who had the task of reading every military order issued to his army. If the soldier in question did not understand the order, Napoleon would re-write it until he did. This gentleman was referred to in the French Army as "Napoleon's Idiot". Senior leaders will find themselves in a very complex and highly responsible position where they can no longer state objectives and task directly to subordinates on a face-to-face basis. While their plans and policies influence their subordinates, they find themselves in an indirect leadership or management role. Now they must rely on the elements of effective communication, be cohesive, concise and brief to be sure everyone understands their verbal actions. Senior Leaders must develop both a mission and vision statement for their organization, and should understand the difference between the two. The mission is what the organization does on a daily basis. What product and service does it deliver? Vision is what the organization will look like in the future. Strategic plans should be developed with milestones and measures to support the accomplishment of the vision. Vision is the primary task of senior management! You would be surprised at the number of organizations in this country that have no idea or plan for their future past next Wednesday. To unlock the door to a vision, one must use the key of imagination. If one cannot image then one cannot visualize.

An example of what a lack of good vision on the part of senior level leadership can do to deter a successful organization is the railroads. This illustration is one to which everyone can easily relate. In the early days of the railroad someone at the senior level had a vision of faster, more comfortable trains. Great sums of money were spent to achieve this objective as the speed and carrying capacity of trains doubled, even tripled. The early "iron horse" steam engine has been surpassed by diesel and electric locomotives, which in some countries have reached speeds of 250 miles per hour. Today passengers travel in well-lighted, heated, and air-conditioned coaches. Freight hauling is accomplished primarily using the piggyback concept—a combination of the train/truck method of material moving and handling. But with all of this innovation why is it that so many railroads have gone out of business; what went wrong? The answer is clear and simple—no vision or poor vision! Senior level leaders at the railroad could not overcome the paradigm that they would always move passengers and freight by train. If they had possessed vision in depth, the early leaders of the railroads would have become involved in aviation, and today would own most of the airlines. Think about that, the New York Central Airlines, or the Pennsylvania Airline, this is what futurists call thinking outside of the box. Most ideas like this come from people that are new to or are outside of the organization. This is generally due to the fact that most people inside an organization are just too close to the problem and too set in their thinking. There are many lessons to be taken from this example. Senior level managers of major oil companies should take heed of the decline of the railroads. Major oil companies should be leading the charge to develop alternative sources of energy other than oil, if they want to survive into the future. Maybe Standard Oil for example should change its name to Standard Energy, and their thinking right along with the name.

Let us now look at a positive example of how thinking outside of the box and vision in depth can produce productive and positive effects. More than sixty years ago, in the dark era of Nazi Germany, the German military developed a concept called "Blitzkrieg", a German word that means, "Lightning War". This concept was way ahead of its time. The concept called for air and land forces to work together, with aircraft for the first time acting as long range artillery. It employed the use of fast moving armor and mechanized forces moving across the ground rapidly behind a shield of artillery and air cover. This was a far cry from the tactics of World War I and the concept of trench warfare. The German's also pioneered the use of airborne forces (paratroopers), which allowed them to hit the enemy behind their front lines in great mass. Because it worked the German

Army overran Europe in a few months. Once again, an excellent example of thinking outside of the box.

While all of this was occurring, in America another visionary warrior was watching and learning from the Germans. His name was General George S. Patton, old "Blood and Guts', as his troopers called him. Patton had vision in depth, reading many of the writings of the German generals that developed "Blitzkrieg", the Lightning War. He knew that modern tank and air power would change the face of war forever. This was a real paradigm shift for an individual that had started his career in the horse cavalry.

If one studies Patton, they will quickly see the source of his vision. He had an active and vivid imagination. He was an avid reader of military battle history. He actually believed that he was reborn from ancient times, reincarnated. His readings made him a twentieth-century man with a two thousand year old mind. One might question Patton's sanity, but history shows that his creativity and imagination came from the vast amount of knowledge he had processed into his mind through reading. He applied his own version of lighting war using the concept of the armor spearhead in 1944 during his famous drive across Europe, defeating the German Army.

Imagination is the foundation of vision, developed through reading. You cannot develop great vision if your mind is a blank page.

To lead, one must visualize and imagine! To develop imagination, it is important to read the thoughts of others, not necessarily to copy them but to improve on them. To be a great leader and visionary one must be a great reader.

Always remember that to make a vision a reality, senior leaders must develop a game plan, establish standards and rules, priorities, and develop milestones to measure success. They must allow time to reflect and consider the influence of their personal factors.

The process begins when they use their imagination to develop the vision, and then apply sound management principles in developing their game plan. The game plan is then routed to subordinates at all levels through the use of effective communications. The senior leaders cannot rest after this has been accomplished. They must outwardly lead the charge and follow-up! Also, staff' members must be held accountable for accomplishing the stated objectives/milestones.

Some individuals may not understand after reading this chapter if they are a senior leader. If you set at the top of the decision matrix you are the senior leader of your organization. This rule applies if you are the CEO of General Motors or you own your own business and employ fifteen people. Always think outside of the box. Actively seek input from you customers and workers on how to improve your organization. Always remember that the best ideas for improvement come from people with a fresh view of your organization.

CHAPTER 4

Principles Of Good Leaders

In all of my studies of leadership, nothing more defines the principles that good leaders should adhere to then the "Seven Principles of the Japanese Martial Arts" also referred to as the Bushido or Samurai Code". But I find in the Bushido Code, as is the cases with many of the Worlds great religions a common morale bond.

Here are the Principles of the Samurai Code:

Chugi—DUTY AND LOYALTY
Gi—JUSTICE AND MORALITY
Makoto—COMPLETE SINCERITY/TRUTHFULNESS
Rei—POLITE COURTESY
Jin—COMPASSION
Yu—HEROIC COURAGE
Meiyo—HONOR

I find it no surprise that in 1990 the United States Army adopted what it refers to, as it's seven core values for its warriors. That code mirrors the principles listed above!

The Samurai for eleven hundred years served and protected the Japanese people, the word Samurai in Japanese means to serve. They were not mindless mercenaries that fought for money; they served a lord or land baron called a Shogun. Their entire way of life was dedicated to the art of war. To them honor and creditability was everything! If a Samurai told someone something their honesty was never in question, they were men of honor.

In modern Japan today, as in ancient Japan, there are still two distinct classes of people, the Samurai class and the common people. The Samurai in ancient Japan were the nobility; this is still true in modern Japan. Most of the major Japanese businesses are owned and run by the Samurai class. I think it is important to look at how the business leaders of one of our major competitors in the World market place conduct their lives and manage their organizations. We should examine the code that they live by compared to the code many American business leaders follow. How would your boss or CEO measure up against the Samurai code? How do you? Are you saying to yourselves that to compare business people to warriors or war to business is insane? But think about this, every business is at war on a daily basis with their competitors, who would put them out of business in an instant if the opportunity, arrived. In 2009, when Toyota was having a major problem with their vehicles self-accelerating do you think Ford, Chrysler and General motors were sorry to see this happening? They were overjoyed. <u>Business is War!</u> But as in war there is a code of conduct you should follow. In your personal life and business I highly recommend the Principles of the Samurai code. Think about posting the code in your office to remind yourself and everyone you interact with what is at the core of your very soul.

In the next chapter I will discuss the characteristic of all successful leaders, and once again you will see traces of the Samurai code. It is important not that you are just a successful business warrior, but also an ethical one. This is a major issue in American business today; there are no ethics, and no code. Like the Army, American business should start looking at posting their core values. Perhaps then, America would start regaining some of its former greatness. I believe the war of business is one that we are losing everyday on the battlefield of the World market.

In closing, I must tell you something that I just read in my local newspaper. It appears that there is a strong possibility that much of the natural gas that is coming out of the Marcella Shale deposit in Northern Pennsylvania may eventually be liquefied and sold to China and Japan. What are we doing to ourselves? Where is our code? What does it matter if this drilling operation creates thousands of jobs if we give away this valuable resource to our chief competitors on the World stage?

CHAPTER 5

Fourteen Characteristics Of Successful Leaders

Several years ago the military conducted a study regarding what was it that all successful leaders had in common. They discovered that history's famous and successful leaders shared fourteen common characteristics. All of them shared these character traits; rather they had been successful in politics, business or the military. I taught a lesson on these characteristics to many future military leaders during my long career. They are not listed in any order of importance, because in fact, they are all equally important. As we go through the characteristics note the appearance of some of the threads of the Samurai Code. The Fourteen Characteristic are as follows:

- **BEARING**—Is the way you carry yourself, walk, talk, stand, and sit; you're dress and your mannerisms. The appearance of a leader and the way they carry themselves is very important. In the first thirty seconds that you initially meet an individual, the majority of your impression of that person is formulated. During my career I served as Chief of the Security Force at

BOB DANMYER

Fort Detrick, Maryland. I used to tell my officers over and over that their individual bearing and appearance reflected on everyone on the force. In many cases good bearing has prevented the use of force in an aggravated situation. Stand tall and walk like you have a purpose were words that I heard over and over again when I was in Officer Candidate School at Fort Benning, Georgia. Those words have stayed with me all of my adult life. Always be mindful of your bearing and how you conduct yourself.

- **COURAGE**—Means to be fearless and brave! It has been said that courage is mastery of your fear. It is easy to understand why combat leaders must have courage; warriors will not follow a coward. But why is courage necessary to be successful in business. Simple, you must have the courage to make tough decisions, and stand up for your people, no matter what the personal cost. Think about this scenario, you are a one hundred a twenty pound female supervisor, in charge of a manufacturing operation. One of your female employees tells you that Big Mike, the outlaw biker that works with her is sexually harassing her on a daily basis. This guy is three hundred and twenty one pounds, six foot four and eats nails for lunch. Well guess by law who has to do something to back Mike down, all one hundred and twenty pounds of you. Think this will take courage, have I made my point! Let me be perfectly clear on another point gentlemen, courage is not just a male characteristic. Many times I have seen some outstanding women display great courage. If you think this is not so guys try delivering an eight-pound baby for example. Most women are just born naturally courageous. Always remember courage is just the ability to manage your fear. How you do that at times can be your greatest challenge in life.

- **DECISIVENESS**—As per Webster's it is the ability to arrive at a solution. The Union came very close to losing the Civil War because the Commander of the Army of the Potomac in 1862, General George McClellan was indecisive; he was known to be to analytical. At the Fort Benning, Georgia Officer Candidate School there was a saying, "Do something even if it is wrong". This statement is never more applicable then when an emergency occurs. Indecisiveness can cost lives, money and the loss of respect for a leader. On the other hand you should be cautioned to think out your decision carefully. But, once you have all of the facts, make a decision.

- **DEPENDABILITY**—If people cannot count on you to be punctual, you will fail, in both life and your career in business. It is that simple! Also, always remember that your word should be your bond! If you say you are going to do something and you have given your word, make sure it happens or die trying.

- **ENDURANCE**—Is the ability to withstand stress. If you are not doing it now I would highly recommend that you get yourself into good physical condition. If you look at most successful leaders you will find that they all have daily exercise programs. Good physical conditioning leads to good mental conditioning. The best way to not get hired for a job is to go to the interview looking out of shape. This is especially true if you are middle-aged; the truth hurts I know, but there it is!

- **ENTHUSIASM**—Is having an intense feeling for a subject. How can you expect your employees to get excited about their work if you never do? Never be negative around your people, your job as a leader is not to de-energize your employees but to electrify them about their work. This task becomes much harder when things are not going well. But a positive attitude can be infectious, and can go a long way in turning things around. Negativity is a fatal disease that will destroy everything it touches.

- **INITIATIVE**—Means to follow through with energy, or take the first step. How many businesses and life ventures have failed because a leader has failed to take the initiative. Once again there is something that has stayed with me since my days at Fort Benning Officer Candidate School. It may be deep, but it goes like this, "Upon the sands of time lie bleaching the bones of thousands, who upon the eve of victory stopped to rest and in doing so died". Basically they gave up the initiative!

- **INTEGRITY**—Webster's Dictionary says that the meaning of this word is firm adherence to a code or a standard of values. How about a leader's adherence to honesty. Commitment to telling the truth, no matter how painful. It is said that if you tell one lie that you will have to tell ten more to cover up the real truth. If you want proof that this is true just look at what happens when a public official is caught breaking the people's trust. In the past thirty years how many times have you seen this played out on the national news? How can anyone follow someone that has no integrity and trust anything they say or do? How many times have you seen supervisors tell an employee that they are going to follow-up on a problem with no intention of doing it? So how does that work, well one employee tells another, who tells ten more, and soon the entire plant knows the boss has no integrity. In industry employees are fired for taking five dollars worth of material while supervisors are stealing the company blind on a daily basis, and everyone knows it. How, by getting so called government jobs made up in the weld or carpenter shop for their homes or trucks, where is the integrity! How many times have you seen raises frozen for state or federal workers, and the politicians vote themselves a nice pay increase. The lack of integrity in organizational leaders will tear apart the very fabric of any operation. As a person or a leader never lose your integrity if you want to maintain your effectiveness and peace of mind! Only a coward lies, many times it will take courage to tell the truth.

- **JUDGMENT**—is the ability to decide. Before you decide get all the facts and always make fair judgments. Another good rule to follow when making a decision is, "If it does not feel right, don't do it".

- **JUSTICE**—Once again Webster's says that justice is the conformity to morale righteousness. Leaders must in today's business world treat everyone equally. It is just against the law to do it any other way.

- **KNOWLEDGE**—You cannot lead any element of an organization if you do not understand the technical side of the operation. It is important that you are always technically proficient or have a sound understanding of the elements that you supervise. This is why they don't hire a mechanic to run a hospital.

- **LOYALTY**—means to be attached to someone or something, not to cheat! Loyalty is a two way street, and it has to be earned and can never truly be dictated. As a leader you must earn your peoples loyalty. I think that most people that read this statement understand this as a basic rule of life. But there is another kind of loyalty that we do not always understand; it is loyalty to your orders and job instructions. When a superior tells you to do something do it, be loyal to the directive. There will be times this will be much more difficult than others. It is said that if you cannot follow orders and directives, you will never get into a position to give them. Always think about loyalty to your directives, yourself and your people!

- **TACT**—is the ability to appreciate the delicacy of a subject and to do and say the kindest thing. (As per Webster's Dictionary). I have seen people that could have been the plant manager. I have seen people that could have been the

Chief Executive Office (CEO) of the Corporation. I have seen people that could have advanced to the upper levels of the military. But they lacked one thing, TACT! The higher you go up the leadership ladder the more tact you will need to be successful. I recommend that you start developing tact while you reside at the bottom, it will pay big dividends in the future. Always tell it like it is, but be tactful.

- **UNSELFISHNESS**—Means to put others ahead of yourself. A good leader does not live in luxury while his employees and people are suffering in poverty. Or give him or herself a big raise when no one in the organization has had one for two years. Or puts out a mandate canceling all vacations for economic reasons, then leaves on a two-week vacation to Spain. Or take from those that do not have it to give! Always remember the golden rule, "Do unto others, as you would have them do unto you". Treat your people the way you would like to be treated ALWAYS!!!!!

To my surprise a characteristic that did not make the list was self-discipline.

Without self-discipline, which is the key to adhering to the characteristic and principles in the two previous chapters, how can you ever hope to succeed as a good leader or person? Self-discipline is the voice in your head that keeps you on track. You know that voice that tells you what is right and wrong when Satan starts whispering in your ear.

In closing this chapter, I am compelled to point out the parallels between the "Fourteen Characteristics of Successful

Leaders", and the "Samurai Code". Or other codes that address human behavior, like the "United States Army's Core Values" or how about the "Ten Commandments", the latter of which has been with us for several thousand years. Morality is a huge part of being a good leader. You must follow the codes of morality if you hope to have a <u>long</u> and successful career.

CHAPTER 6

Understanding People

This chapter will deal with something that is seldom discussed in the leadership circles. So why devote an entire chapter to such a delicate subject. The answer is simple; one of the greatest failures of leadership is an inability to interact properly with other human beings. Why is this? The reason is most leaders don't understand themselves, so how are they going to understand other people? Do you think that it is an accident that in order to get a degree in business, you are required to take and pass both sociology and psychology courses.

One of the many resources available to us to clarify personalities and develop relationship awareness is psychological profiling. While there are many psychological profile-testing instruments available to organizations that will analyze an employee's personality, few are ever used. The most popular one in use today is the Myers-Briggs; but there is also the Keirsey-Bates. All of these tools work by asking a series of specific questions on a variety of scenarios. The way you answer the questions determines the make-up of your personality. Many personnel specialist and managers use these tools to determine if they are hiring the right personality type for the job in question.

For example if you were hiring a sales manager, you would want someone that was very extroverted and aggressive. If you were looking for a research scientist you might want someone that was more introverted and analytical. For a nursing position, police officer or fireman's job you might want someone that cares for people.

Personality analysis's tools are also great for teambuilding. For any team to be successful you should have a mixture of personalities, this helps the team to maintain balance and focus.

In training sessions to illustrate the three major personality classifications list above I have used the following examples: The Lion, for the assertive/aggressive personality, the Saint Bernard, for the caring personality and the Owl for the analytical personality. Can you image a team made up of all Lions; they would waste a lot of time fighting for power and control. A team of all Saint Bernard's would focus entirely on the effect a solution to a problem would have on people. A team of Owls could never come to a decision without taking the time to analyze the problem, always asking where is the data. Owls also can get stuck in analysis paralysis.

In a mixed team of Lions, Saint Bernard's and Owls one personality tends to keep the other on the right tract. For example the Lions who are the drivers on a team want to charge in and affect a solution. The Owls say we need to slowdown and look at the data before we make a decision. Saint Bernard's say before we do this what effect will it have on people? A mixed team always comes up with the best solutions to problems, admittedly after a little turmoil.

On the Internet you will find the web site of a worldwide company called the Personal Strengths Publishing Company. The web address is: http:/www.personalstrenghts.com. I have in the past attended several of their training sessions. Their copyrighted material is in my opinion the best Relationship Awareness tool I have ever seen. The tool is called the Self Deployment Inventory (SDI). SDI uses the colors red, blue and green to color code personality types. The color red would represent the Lion, blue the Saint Bernard and green the Owl. SDI is easy to understand and as you can see the illustration that I used with the animals mirrors SDI. SDI training teaches the relationship awareness of all personality types and the proper way to interact with those personalities. For example Owls do not like to be given deadlines on making decisions without looking at all the available information on the subject. Lions sometimes tend to get upset with analytical people (Owls) that want to go slow. I have worked with several organizations that after going through SDI training have put the personality color code of every individual in the organization on their nametags. This tool gives employees an idea of what to do and say, or not do and say when involved in communication with their teammates. Can you image having this advantage when communicating with your supervisor. SDI also will give you an idea of how you react to conflict or aggression. All people react differently, it is not the same with everyone, some people get assertive and some retreat into an analytical mode?

To detail in this chapter all of the specifics of the Myers-Briggs, the Keirsey-Bates or the Self Deployment Inventory (SDI) would violate copyrighted material. Therefore, I urge you to look into the systems listed above. More information can be found on such tools in most local libraries and on the Internet. I highly recommend watching the very informative video on the Personnel Strengths Publishing Companies website. It says it all.

Give yourself a tremendous edge in understanding yourself and other people by learning about and using these great instruments. It is well worth the time and trouble.

CHAPTER 7

Interacting With Your Most Valuable Resource

So what is your greatest resource? The answer is simple your customers and employees. You would not believe the number of people in management positions that do not believe this and will answer the "stockholders". You can have the greatest source of raw material in the World. You can have state of the art machinery. But without customers to whom to sell your products, you have no business. Without well-trained and content employees to run the machinery and process the raw material into finished products there is no business. There is one rule that I was taught early in my management career, treat people the way you would like to be treated. In the movie "Wall Street" the main charter Gordon Greco says that greed is good. Did you ever think that that attitude is exactly what is wrong with America today, maybe even the World? If you have seen the movie look at what happens to old Gordon. He winds up in jail. You want another example, how about Bernie Madoff. Look at all the people his greed hurt with his 50 billion dollar Ponzi scheme. Madoff had more money than he could spend, but still wanted more. In 2009 he was sent to a Federal prison, where he will live the rest of his life. Still think greed is good?

Let's look at how to treat your customers, but more importantly what causes a business to loose customers. First, a customer is always right. Never allow yourself to get into an argument with a customer. It can be the kiss of death for your business. Spend as much time as you can with your customers, get to know them personally. Find out how many children they have. Are they in college? What is their wife's first name? Does she work? In other words, learn about your customers at a personal level. Here is something to think about. In Japan a great deal of business is conducted on the golf course. Think about it. Golf courses are beautiful and a completely different atmosphere than a stuffy office or interview room. Good salesmen make their customers their friends, even when they are hard to like.

Finally, never create a sense of fear in a customer. For example a critical shipment from your company is due to the customer. Without it their business comes to a stop and creates unnecessary expenses. I guarantee that if you do this enough the customer will very quickly find another supplier. One of the best salesman that I ever dealt with kept an emergency supply of his product in the garage for his customers. If something went wrong with a shipment he could load it on a truck and delivery it within an hour. One day there was a truck accident on the local freeway and it stopped a vital shipment. I was running out of product, the operation was going to shutdown. It would have taken twenty-four hours to get a new shipment from the plant in New Jersey delivered to my plant in Maryland. When I called the salesman he said he was renting a truck and would have his product delivered in fifty-five gallon drums to my plant in two hours. The drums weighed five hundred pounds each, but he manhandled them onto the truck at his house. He saved me, saved my career; and I was his customer and friend forever.

Now for your employees. First and foremost you must satisfy their basic needs. If you are not paying them enough to fill their bellies and put a roof over their heads you are failing them. If you do not believe this, look up and study a gentleman by the name of Abraham Harold Maslow. Specifically his ladder on the hierarchy of needs, more commonly know as "Maslow's Ladder". Maslow's studies basically concluded that until individuals basic needs are satisfied human beings will never expire to bigger and better things on the ladder of life. Good employers should strive to create the best possible work environment they can. It should be clean, clear and harassment free! Treat all employees fairly regardless of race, religion, creed or national origin. In America that is the law it is called the "Equal Opportunity Act"; there can be no other way.

Never discipline an employee in public. Public discipline is embarrassing and it will cause the employee to fight back out of pure pride, and it will cause other employees to lose respect for you.

Many leaders like to do "Mass Ass Chewing's" to relieve their stress when things are not going well. You may know what I am talking about. That is where the boss calls the entire organization together to tell them how badly they are doing and they must do better. This solves nothing, and generally demoralizes people, making matters worse. If things are not right in an organization use the problem solving process: Define the problem. Determine the solution. Employ the solution. Analyze the effect. Let me give you an example of what I am talking about. For twenty-four years I was a Production Manager for a fortune five hundred company and an officer in the National Guard. I managed four separate departments located in a thirty eight thousand square foot area. One of the departments was turning out poor quality products. So I decided to talk to all of the shifts in the operation using the 'Mass Ass Chewing" method. When I got to the second shift I gave my rather diplomatic but hard line speech. When I had finished I was approached by one of my most outstanding machine operators. She told me that she took a great deal of pride in what she did, and asked why did I have to hear all of that; she had a point. Next she said that I should pin down the specific cause of the problem by reviewing the operation records that were kept on all the machines. I immediately apologized to her for my stupid mistake and promised her I would not repeat the same mistake with the third shift. But, that I would tell them that we had a problem and I was reviewing operator records in order to determine a solution. I also asked them to help me in any way they could and asked their opinion on a solution. The next day I pulled the records and found that out of almost fifty operators, two were creating all the problems. I counseled the operators in question and asked them how I could help improve their performance. They quickly pointed out some very real mechanical problems with their machines. Once these deficiencies were corrected the problem went away in a matter of days. What can I say, I was young and made a mistake, but I learned from it and so can you.

Reward your people when they do something special. People like to stand out in the crowd, (more Maslow). Create an awards and recognition program. Give them something they can display and be proud of for the rest of their lives, and it does not have to be money.

It would be regrettable if I did not point out a rule you should always follow when counseling employees. Protect yourself. Never counsel an employee alone. Always have a third party present, especially when counseling a member of the opposite sex. I have known a couple of outstanding individuals that made this mistake and ended their careers. If you violate this rule, you may find that your world can get real ugly.

In closing this chapter, let me say that a good leader can make an employee really enjoy coming to work. A bad leader can do just the opposite and make the employee hate the thought of walking through the door of the building. I believe that managers who make life miserable for their employees have a responsibility to a higher authority. One day they will answer to their God for the abuse they have inflected on people. The one consistent thing you can count on in this life and the next is, "What goes around, comes around". Think about it!

CHAPTER 8

How To Choose The Right Leader

History has shown that if you surround yourself with the right people you will be successful. This can be true even if you are not the strongest leader yourself, or weak in some areas of your business. So what is the key to making the right choice when selecting the next shop foreman, plant manager, maintenance leader or office manager? I believe the answer to that question is simple: get the best value you can for your dollar. When it comes to people there is no substitute for a quality individual who is technically proficient in their field of endeavor. Too many employers will shop for a manager using the frugal side of their nature. I would rather pay a little more for a quality person that does the job right the first time, than someone that works cheap, but does nothing well. Over time you will pay more to have their work corrected. You may even be required to hire a second person to help with their workload. Also, poor service to your customers will affect the success of your business. In the long run have you saved anything? A quality person, besides doing it right the first time, will always go the extra mile to accomplish a task. For example stay late when there is a deadline to meet or work on Saturday when the need arises.

Let me give you a couple examples of where I am going with all of this. You are looking for a new sales manager at your auto dealership. Sales are way down and the current sales manager tends not to come to work all the time. You believe he may even have a drinking problem. He just cannot get to work before ten in the morning and is out sick on Monday many times. Does all of that sound familiar to any of you? Also, there is no one currently working at your dealership remotely qualified for the position. Turnover in the past year has been really high within the current sales force and none of the current salesman have management experience. Of all the people that you have interviewed for the position you have narrowed it down to two people. Both candidates you are looking at as a replacement have interviewed well. Candidate number one is young and has been out of college about two years. He has a Masters in Business Administration (MBA) and has had three jobs in the last two years. He said he was very successful at his last job, but can produce nothing to prove it. When asked about the mobility in his career, he has responded that he has moved around a great deal in an effort to improve his salary and position. He requires a yearly salary of $80,000 per year. Candidate number two has been in sales for the past 23 years, with the same car dealership. He worked his way up from salesman to sales manager in four years, went to night school and managed to get a bachelors degree in business, while raising a family. It took him eight years to complete his education on the G.I. Bill, but he did finish. He has done well at his current dealership and can produce several certificates of achievement as proof of his success. Unfortunately, the dealership at which he has been working at is going out of business. The current owner

49

is retiring and their sponsor, General Motors, is cutting back on their dealerships. He is middle aged and has some gray hair, but appears to be a high-energy person. Because he has children in college and a mortgage, he is asking for $115,000 per year. Who would you hire? I can tell you that this scenario is repeated everyday around this great country. Generally, the gentleman fresh out of college that can be hired for $35,000 less a year will get the job. With no proven record of success or loyalty to an employer, he will get the job. Simply because he is younger and will work for a lower salary. As for the guy that won't get the job he has survived in sales for 24 years. Do you think he is good? Thirty five thousand dollars is a drop in the bucket when you look at the dollars a good sales manager can generate for a business. Your business is already in trouble because of a low quality individual and you hire another one because you are frugal. Have you ever heard this one; "You get what you pay for".

Let me give you another good example of where I am going will all of this. The private security business is an industry that is really challenged by their clients. Every business wants good security, but because security is non-productive and pure overhead, no one wants to pay more than they have to for security personnel. This is the reason that you see some sorry looking individual in a baggy uniform guarding the plant and the five hundred souls that work inside. For a few more dollars you can have a retired Navy Seal or police officer that will do the job right and protect your employees properly. Remember, once again, you get what you pay for and there is no "free lunch".

While all of this addresses the hiring of a new manager, what about promotion from within? Generally, we have a tendency to promote the individual with the most seniority. This is real true in union shops and businesses. I am not downing unions; they have surely had their place in American history. Here is the problem with only using seniority. The most senior and best mechanic may not make the best maintenance leader. While they may be a good mechanic, they may have no organizational, leadership or people skills. You set them up for failure when you promote them into a position they will wind up hating, because they lack skills necessary to do the job. Look at everyone that is eligible, you can always train someone in a process or profession. You cannot train in personality. Personality is something that is set in place by the time we are seven years old. Old Joe may be a great top mechanic, but could not organize his way out of a paper bag, and is terrible when interacting with people. There is a theory called the "Peter Principle", that states, "That everyone will eventually rise to his or her own level on incompetence". My experience with individuals that have suffered the effect of the principle is their failure is generally due to personality issues. Like not being able to interact well with other people!

While I have given you just a few examples of what not to do, what are the rules you should follow when promoting or hiring a new manager? Here are the ones I have used over the years:

1. Individual should be well spoken and interview well, answering all questions accurately and in an intelligent manner,
2. They should present a good appearance, clean, neat and well groomed.

3. Should be dressed appropriately for the position they will fill.
4. Be on time for the interview!
5. Be able to prove they are qualified for the position.
6. Do they appear to be well organized?
7. Eager to accept the position!
8. Have a clean background, no major credit or criminal problems. Run a check on line, but only with their written permission.
9. Process good people skills.
10. Have some responsibility in life, like a family, buying a home, etc.
11. Are they working to improve themselves by going to night school, etc?
12. Be morally sound with good principles.
13. Do they have any leadership training or background, like being in the military?
14. They should have nothing negative to say about a past or present employer.
    (If they do, this could be a red flag)!
15. Are they likable?
16. Act confident!
17. Are they physically and mentally active outside of work; i.e.: have a hobby, read, golf, hunt, run, workout at the gym, etc?
18. Are they loyal to the instructions they are given?
19. Are they active in their community or place of worship?
20. Do you feel you can work with them?

21. Does this individual have a track record of going the extra mile, work overtime, etc?

Remember in Chapter Six I discussed some personality analysis tools that can help you get some answers to the questions above like the Kersey-Bates, Myers-Briggs and the Self Deployment Inventory (SDI). Also, remember that not hiring or promoting someone based solely on race, creed, religion, national origin, age or sex, is against the law in America. Also, think long and hard about hiring relatives, particularly if they are not good workers. Promoting a relative that works for you over others can make for some interesting problems. Many companies will not let relatives work for relatives, because of the problems that can occur from such an issue. Many more will not hire the close relatives of current employees.

The bottom line on all of this is always, "Hire the best person for the job". This is the only way to truly succeed in life and business. Never let prejudice get in the way of your final hiring decision; it is just bad business and against the law.

CHAPTER 9

Teambuilding

Good teambuilding is important for a leader to be successful. One of the challenges in writing this chapter is that there are hundreds of tools available to help a leader with this task. The majority of them are under copyright and you tread on dangerous legal ground when you write about them. However, I can give you a few tips and tell you where to find the information necessary to accomplish good teambuilding. I learned from my football playing days that the team concept is the best way to solve problems. Unfortunately many people that advance into leadership positions feel that they have to solve all the organization's problems on their own. This thought process is often referred to as the "One Smart Man Principle". An empowered team will always come up with a better solution to a problem because they employ the collective thinking process. I have also found that leaders who are insecure in their positions will never empower their people and will try to manager everything on their own. Three heart attacks later they finally learn this is not the way to lead.

A good team should always have a balance of personalities. A team that is not structured this way does not make balanced decisions. Remember what I wrote about in Chapter VI, "Understanding Yourself and Others". A good team should be a mix of Owls. Lions and Saint Bernard's. Additionally, when a team is formed to solve a problem, the tendency is for the members to go right into the problem-solving mode. You must go slowly before you can go fast. To better understand what I am talking about, go on line to a search engine and type in Process Improvement Process. You will find that this model is an excellent problem-solving tool. When using this tool remember to follow all the steps, never skip over one. Your team should have a mission statement that is results oriented. Everyone should understand the roles and responsibilities they have on the team. Before a team meeting an agenda should be published so everyone knows what is being discussed. This allows members to properly prepare for the meeting. The team leader should allow ideas to flow and not dominate the meeting. Try brainstorming. This is a good way to get people thinking. A simple form of brainstorming is to go around the room and ask people to present their ideas on how to solve a particular problem. If you write them down on a board or on butcher paper in the front of the room you will have a written record to refer to during and after the meeting. These notes will also help when it is time to do minutes for the meeting. Minutes should always be done after every meeting or team building session in order to maintain a living record for future meetings. It is an excellent idea to establish a time limit for the meeting and set meeting rules; that once again should be captured on paper. Two meeting rules that I would highly recommend is, "Stay on Time: and "No War Stories". A war story is when team members start talking about how we did it back in 1996. These stories tend to draw out the meeting and waste time. Finally, always determine how to track your progress. The best way to measure progress will almost always be statistical data.

In closing I hope that these thoughts and tips have been helpful. As a leader you must know how to run a successful meeting or teambuilding session. The local library and Internet has hundreds of books and articles on this subject. I hope all of this is helpful and good luck with your teambuilding process.

CHAPTER 10

Get Your Tickets Punched

Some readers may not be familiar with the term, "Get your tickets punched". This term is used all the time in the military. It means you must always strive to obtain the necessary credentials to rise to the next level of your profession. The one regret that I had in the years that I spent in the business world was I was never motivated by my company to advance my education. This is just the opposite in the military and that is a good thing, particularly when you have to finally leave the service and go back into the job market. In situations where you have the required certifications for the promotion posted on the bulletin board, you may be selected over other candidates, because you have those certifications. The other candidates do not! In other words you've, "gotten your tickets punched". They have not. You should always be working on improving your resume! Believe me employers like people who are going to night school or taking a special technical course to improve themselves. In the military you are required to complete certain schools to advance to the next rank. Also, you could be promoted over individuals that have been on the promotion list longer than you have. Because they have not worked to obtain the certifications required to move forward.

You may have picked up welding skills by just hanging around the welding shop at lunchtime; and you have gotten good at it, but have you gotten certified? This could make a big difference when the next welders position becomes available at ten dollars an hour more than your current salary. Additionally, a situation may arise where a new contract requires that only certified welders may work on that particular project. If you are in the medical field certifications are updated yearly and are crucial for promotion, hiring and to hold a current position. My wife is a Registered Nurse (RN) and she is constantly going to school. She does this to stay up to date on new practices, which change rapidly in modern medicine. Additionally, without continuously improving herself she could be dismissed from her current position.

Going back to school can be very difficult in later life. Everyone knows how hard it is to work all day and then go to night school. I obtained both of my degrees and some of my military certifications this way. But I can also tell you that the entire time that I was doing this I had a sense that things would improve in my life. It eventually paid off and was well worth the time and effort.

I think by now you should understand what I am trying to say. Find out what you have to do at your company to advance. Also, if you are working to improve yourself by going to night school for example, make sure your supervisors are aware of this. Even if you don't have the degree necessary for that new promotion, if you are working on it, the effort counts for something. Remember, for an individual to have an education is good. For an individual to have experience is good! However, alone the two may not count for much, combined they are solid gold. One of my best friends is stuck right now in a plant manager's position and cannot advance because he lacks a four-year college education. He is however, excellent at what he does! On the other hand I have another younger friend that has the education but because she lacks experience cannot obtain a teaching position. Think about both of these cases and get your tickets punched. Go to school at night if necessary, work for nothing to get experience if you have to, but get your tickets punched. Years ago an old friend told me I should always remember; "The lead sled dog always has the best view". If you are not a leader on your current work team I am sure you understand the message my friend was sending.

In closing, remember; never stop the process of continually improving yourself and everything around you. The Japanese have a word for this practice, and it is call "Kaizen". Kaizen is the key to being successful in everything you strive for in life; practice it everyday.

CHAPTER 11

Staying In Shape

In his book, "The 7 Habits of Highly Effective People", Dr. Stephen R. Covey sites exercise, along with meditation or prayer and social interaction as some of the key elements of Habit 7, entitled, "Sharpen the Saw". I would highly recommend reading Dr. Covey's book to learn about all seven habits. The book is excellent. The good doctor was right on target with his assessment. Every successful leader that I have ever known generally has an exercise plan. President Barrack Obama for example loves to play golf and basketball and his predecessor jogged to stay in shape. I have just reached my seventieth birthday and still play golf on Mondays then go to the gym on Wednesdays and Fridays to walk, bike and lift weighs. Exercise reduces stress, improves your overall health and increases your mental capacities. Heaven knows you need the latter to succeed as a leader! Stress will also cause you to gain weight! One of the most stressful jobs that I ever held caused me to gain twenty pounds over a five-year period. Within weeks of leaving the position, and without dieting, I lost most of that twenty pounds. Generally people in leadership positions are under more stress than the employees they supervise. You must exercise to mange the stress or it will hurt you, physiologically speaking. Maybe even kill you! Many people that I know in leadership and management positions will say, "I just don't have time to exercise". To those individuals I say, "You will have time after your first heart attack".

Making the time for exercise may not be as difficult as you think. For years I went to the gym three days a week at the end of the workday. Suddenly, I woke up one day and I was a single parent. Now I had to rush home after work to recover a nine year old from the babysitter. At the time I was in the military and had to take a Physical Fitness test once a year, and pass it to keep my job. I could not exercise in the morning because day care centers have set hours that do not start until six thirty or seven A.M., so I started working out on my lunch hour. I still do Physical Training (PT) during the lunch hour even though I am now retired and have no children to pick up from the babysitter. Also, I still work out with a PT partner that I have worked out with for the past eighteen years. Having a PT partner makes working out much easier and I highly recommend that you get one. I would recommend that you do PT a <u>minimum</u> of one hour three times a week. You will notice that I said at a minimum, more is better! Ladies, something to think about: shopping is a form of exercise and is good for you if you don't spend your life savings or go in debt while you do it. My wife has stayed in shape this way for years!

Exercising your mind is also important and cannot be accomplished by watching daytime television. Try playing chess, checkers, or a good game of cards. All of these things will help improve your mental capacities. Any game or hobby that makes you think things out and arrive at a solution can also serve this purpose.

I hope I have made you see the importance of both physical and mental exercise! If you currently do not have a workout or exercise program think about joining a gym. A professional trainer can get you started on the right track. You may ask when is the best time to get started? To that I can only answer, ten minutes after you finish reading this chapter. Just get up and take a walk around the block to get started. It is also important to point out that you should always have a session with your family doctor before you start an exercise program. You should never over do it. You don't have to prove anything to anyone or impress the members of the opposite sex in the gym. They might even laugh at you for trying! Something else that I have practiced over the years is finding quiet time to think and meditate. When times were really tough at work I would do this just to save a piece of my soul for myself. This was a special time of day that belonged only to me. The long drive home from work this can serve that purpose very well.

In closing I hope this short chapter has made you think about the importance of mental and physical exercise and quiet time in your life and career. Good luck with your PT program and may you livelong and prosper.

CHAPTER 12

Getting Along With Your Supervisor

Getting along with your supervisor can at times be really difficult. However, I cannot emphasize how important it is to your career to live up to this challenge. Face it there are some supervisors that are just plain mean. I have worked for a few that fall into that category. However, you can even survive under those types of supervisors if your job performance makes them look good. One of my better supervisors told me that, "It was my job to make him look good and his job to make his supervisor look good". No one can turn a blind eye to good performance. The worst supervisor that ever lived understands they cannot survive if they do not have a staff full of quality people. On the other side of the coin, I will be the first to admit that a good boss makes it a pleasure to go to work everyday. All of that said; let me break this issue down into the following two categories.

1. **The importance of getting along with your supervisor:**

The bottom line is that whether you like your boss or hate your boss; they hold your career in the palm of their hand. Remember, they are the ones that sign and prepare your job evaluations. Those evaluations may determine if you get a raise, keep your job or get promoted. Are you getting the picture? I have known some outstanding civilian supervisors and military officers that had their careers go up in flames because of personality conflicts with their supervisors.

In 2003, I went to work as a Department of Defense (DOD) contractor at Fort Detrick, Maryland. I was the Chief of the Security Force, responsible for securing the perimeter of the installation. To give you an idea of the nature of the work, we accomplished this objective with the help of automatic pistols and shotguns. My personnel were required to undergo 120 hours of training and pass several key tests, like qualifying with their weapons and passing a physical fitness test. This was right after 9/11 and the facility was under a serious threat from a terrorist attack. My primary supervisor, who was an outstanding boss, was located in Virginia. However, at Fort Detrick I answered directly to the Director of Public Safety. He was a tough, performance oriented, retired Army Sergeant. Additionally, he had his doubts that civilian guards could do the job that military personnel had done in the past. After all, a contract guard force was a new experiment, the first of its kind. Many other people at Fort Detrick shared his opinion. I knew the experiment would work. Because for the most part the majority of the force was made up of former military and law enforcement personnel It was important that we succeed. This force was one of a kind. The country was about to go to war and the Army needed their soldiers to fight that war, not guard the Fort. In fact the military unit my guard force replaced went on to fight in Iraq the following year. As the Director of Public Safety, he was a challenge to work with to say the least. But once he realized that I understood he was the boss, and that my people could do the job, our performance won him over to our side. While at times I disagreed with him, I never became confrontational. I also did all I could, within my power, to listen to him and give him what he wanted. Early in my work career I was taught the customer is always right. You should think of your supervisor as a primary customer.

I made a point to have coffee with him in the morning and the other two key members of his management team, the Captain of Police and Fire Chief, both were great people. It took a year, but I earned the right to be part of his team. He went from not liking contract guards to a defender of both the project and me. I started to enjoy working with him, and when he left Fort Detrick in 2007, to go on to better things, I was sorry to see him leave. Since 2003 the DOD has gone on to employ over 3000 contract guards at installations all over the United States. Because Fort Detrick was the first military installation to employ contract guards, many of our operating procedures were used to manage the duplicate forces. The DOD calls the project Force Protection. These guard forces protect the men and women who are charged with protecting this great nation, the United States Military. This was and is still today dangerous work.

2. **Tips for getting along with your supervisor:**
    1. First and foremost, be a performer, there can be no substitute for success.

2. <u>Make your supervisor look good.</u> Support their agenda; make sure they understand that you know you are there to support them on their road to success.

3. If you can spend some social time with the boss. It does not hurt that you know one another on a personal level. However, this cannot be a substitute for performance. This does not mean dating the boss to get ahead. In fact, I would caution you not to do that under any circumstance.

4. Disagree if you feel the boss is wrong, don't be a yes man. But, avoid being confrontational.

5. Always be willing to go the extra mile, work overtime, come in early, stay late, etc.

6. Finally, be loyal to your supervisor and all of his/her directives.

In closing there is one final issue that I feel is important. During your career there will be many battles that you will have to fight with supervisors. I am not talking about the kind where someone is shooting at you. For example, your supervisor might want to eliminate the lunch hour for your department to make it more efficient. Or do something that might increase your operating cost and in your opinion make your operation less efficient. Know and understand when a battle is worth fighting. Fighting every small, unimportant issue that may arise during your time with an organization may detract from the importance of a big issue when it comes along. People may start perceiving you as the boy that cries wolf, or not being a team player and a difficult person with whom to work. Choose your battles very wisely!

Once again, always remember that if you take care of your supervisor they will usually take care of you. If this does not turn out to be the case, maybe it is time to move on.

CHAPTER 13

Supervising In A Union Environment

Supervising in a union work place may not be as difficult as you perceive. In fact, if approached properly it can be easy. Many people, including union members have the wrong perception of the role a union plays in the work place. While I have never been a union member, I have supervised in a union environment.

The American labor movement has had a huge and positive role in the shaping of the American workplace. While this may sound strange coming from someone that spent all of his life in management, it is a historical fact. Unions have at various times in our history accomplished great things, such as improving deplorable working conditions. On the other hand, if a union does not work with a company they can drive it out of business; or worse yet overseas.

Unions represent a variety of people. Like attorneys they cannot always choose whom to defend or not defend. All of the members pay for representation and they expect to get good value for their dollar. Like any functioning organization that sells a service, unions need funds to operate or they go out of business. This is why their members are charged dues.

Needless to say not every work place in this country is union. I have always said that the best employment situation you can have is to have a good employer. One that cares about the welfare of the employees under their charge. If this is not the case more than likely you are going to be unionized. So how does the conversion of a workplace from non-union to a union shop occur? What is the process? When the employees of any organization decide the company is not treating them fairly and they want union representation, they contact a union. Next, a union organizer will start meeting with the employees off the job site. The law states that organizers cannot do their job on company time or company property. The organizer will call for a meeting with the workers, close to the work place. The number of people that attend this meeting will generally help the union decide if organizing the company in question is worth their time and money. Local fire halls and social halls are usually a prime place for these meetings to occur. The organizer will try to rally the workers in attendance to promote the union, and help them organize a campaign. Perhaps by handing out union literature and buttons. This literature cannot be given out on company time. Once the campaign to bring a union into the work place starts, life for management can become real challenging. Besides doing your normal everyday task, you find yourself on one side of a political type of campaign and acting like a politician. You spend a great deal of time giving out company literature informing your employees of all the reasons why they do not need a union. The company will in most cases do all they can to discredit the union. The union will attempt to do the same to the company. It is your typical American political campaign. Depending on the union, the Internet and the public library can be a huge source of negative information on a union.

The soul purpose of the organizing effort is always to get the employees to sign cards calling for an election. If the union gets enough cards from the employees stating they want union representation, the cards are forwarded to the National Labor Relation Board (NLRD). NLRB runs those elections, or the Federal Labor Relations Authority (FLRA) if Federal employees are involved. The purpose of the election is to determine if the majority of the employees want union representation. Because supervisors are considered part of management they are usually not allowed to vote in such an election. I have lived through many union campaigns during my long management career. I can tell you they can become nasty and dangerous. Passions can run high and violence sometimes occurs. In the majority of cases neither the union nor the company encourages violence. But, because of the strong feelings generated between workers that side with the union or the company, it does happen. It is just human nature. The job that puts food on your table is sacred to everyone involved in the campaign and election.

The election is usually conducted on company property and supervised by the NLRB or FLRA. A majority vote is necessary for a win to occur. If the union loses the election they just depart into the sunset and life goes back to normal. If the union wins the election that is a different matter altogether. Then the company and union will set a date to start conducting negotiations to determine the terms of the union contract. Those subsequent negotiations are where the union attempts to satisfy worker grievances with the company. Once this task has been accomplished, the negotiated terms are turned into a binding contract that both parties sign and agree to uphold. Generally, a contract is good for three years. The contract is eventually turned into a pamphlet and both the management team and union members are given copies as a reference guide. Everyone follows the terms of the contract as stated in this pamphlet.

At some point during the time the union negotiates with the company the union members will select shop stewards and a union president. Shop stewards are individuals that represent the interest of the union workers at the local level. There is usually one assigned to each organizational element of a company. Generally this is not a paid position. If the membership is large enough a local union president will be elected. This is usually a paid position. If the local union membership is small in number, the local organizer or regional union representive will serve in this position for several small sites.

So the company has lost the election! You fought hard to keep the union out of your area of supervision. You feel that you were doing a good job of taking care of your workers and don't need a union to help you do your job. If you lost the election something was not right. You need to rethink your position in all of this. First, union or no union you are still the supervisor, plant manager, shop foreman or company owner. None of that has changed. The union has to negotiate for all the concessions it wants from the company for the union membership. If you are a shop manger you still give orders and run the shop. If it is your company, you still own it and all of its resources. In fact if you lighten up a little bit, you may find that the union has just made your job easier in some respects. You now have a specific, detailed set of guidelines on how to interact with you employees. You know the same people that you have known and maybe even been friends with for the last twenty years. The same people that have helped make you successful over the years by doing a great job. So the key to being an effective supervisor in a union environment is the shop steward.

If you have a good shop steward, one that is reasonable and you can work with, this method will work. However, life being what it is, you don't always get such a shop steward. If that is the case, I will pray for you.

During the time that I supervised in a union environment I was lucky to have a good shop steward. I believe the majority of the time you will get a good shop steward. I have found that after the union election is over and it comes time to pick a shop steward the slackers do not want the extra work. Usually, the better people rise to meet this challenge.

This is how I adjusted to my new union environment. If an issue would arise I would get a copy of the union contract out and see if my actions were in line with the terms set down in the contract. Then I would meet with the shop steward to see if they agreed with my actions. If the shop steward did not agree I might adjust my decision, based on the contract. For serious issues that meant time off for the employee, loss of pay or termination, I would have my actions reviewed by the Human Resources Department and get their approval to proceed. This worked. If it were a situation that required the employee be sent from the site immediately, say for example they were fighting. I would send the employee home stating that they were off the site pending a further review of their actions. Never did I use the words fired or terminated. I would then get in touch with Human Resources and the shop steward before a determination of any final action. Following this formula I never had one of my decisions reversed. Yes, it did take a little longer to follow the steps, but in the long run it was worth the time and trouble. It saved everyone a great deal of time, money and embarrassment.

If a matter cannot be settled between a local supervisor and shop steward, or the supervisors superior it goes up to the next level. That level varies from contract to contract. At that next level, usually a settlement meeting occurs between the local union president or regional representative and the companies Human Resources Department. If the issue cannot be resolved there it moves up to a final level, binding arbitration.

Every contract is written differently concerning binding arbitration. For example, the contract may state that a non-biased arbitrator be selected from a list of certified arbitrators. In other contracts it may be sent to the National Labor Relations Board for arbitration. If it is an issue involving Federal employees it would go the Federal Labor Relations Authority. The arbitrator involved in settling the issue may conduct an administrative review of the issue and make a decision. If the issue is serious the arbitrator many conduct a meeting between the union and the company and attempt through mediation to come to a resolution. The decision of the arbitrator is final and both parties must abide by the decision or face fines and legal action. Always remember that solving the problem at the lowest level is the cheapest and most effective way to accomplish resolution.

In summary, remember to always base your action on the tenets of the union contract. Work with your shop steward. Be fair and show no favoritism. Always remember that you are the leader and manager. You are the one in charge, not the union.

CHAPTER 14

Resolving Employee Conflict

In 1987 the military sent me to the Defense Equal Opportunity Management Institute (DEOMI), located at Patrick Air Force Base, Florida. DEOMI was established at Patrick Air Force Base several years ago and is attended by both civilian and military personnel from the entire Department of Defense (DOD). Every branch of the military and every organization in DOD send personnel to DEOMI. Their primary sixteen-week course consists of sociological and psychological education on the diverse issues we confront in our society. In plain English it is a race relation school. Many of the courses address the power of conflict and how it can destroy the cohesiveness of organizations. While in attendance at DEOMI, I recall one of my instructors stating that in the sixties an entire carrier battle group had to turn back to port and away from its mission because of race riots on the lead carrier. It is a safe guess to say, all of this started with a conflict between two sailors.

Some managers think that if you do not address conflict it may go away. I personally saw a commander of a military medical unit have his long career terminated because of such an attitude. Some employee problems may appear to be small to you as a leader, but they may be huge to the employee. If you do not address their problem because you are just too busy, or you think it will go away in time, the employee will find someone who will listen to them. That someone may not be an individual you want interfering in your business. For example, like the company president, the plant manager, the union, or worse an outside investigating agency like the Department of Labor or the Equal Opportunity Commission.

When I was a production manager at Maryland Cup Corporation, in one of the three departments that I supervised, I had two of my better machine operators that just could not work together. In fact, they hated one another. This conflict eventually split the entire first shift of the department in question right down the middle. After trying several times using the method I am about to describe, I finally took some of the heat out of the problem by separating them. I had the shift manager place them on machines at opposite ends of the department, located fifty yards away from one another. The shift manager was also careful not to send them on lunch break at the same time. I have talked to other managers that said this problem would have been better solved by making them work together in the same area and not separating them. Survival situations tend to bring people together. If you do decide to solve the conflict by making the employees in question work in the same area, you need to watch the situation closely.

The method for conflict resolution I am about to describe to you I have used for years to resolve complex issues between large groups and individuals. This is how it works. First, you meet individually with the individuals involved in the conflict, to get a feel for what it will take to resolve the problem. This is where you need to employ effective listening skills. Next you meet with both parties in a quiet location. At the outset of the meeting you establish meeting rules and get everyone in attendance to agree to follow them. Try to make these rules their rules. One rule that must be established and followed is, one-person talks at a time. Without this one rule the meeting can be total chaos. It is always helpful to record the rules and post them. Your job in facilitating the process is not to take sides in the conflict. In other words manage the process, stay out of the content. Also, the one person in the room that cannot lose control of their emotions is you. Stay calm and maintain your cool. I have managed some heated discussion between individuals with just the one-person talks at a time rule. If you trust the process it will work.

If the conflict resolution meeting involves many issues, and you have a large group involved an agenda should be prepared before the meeting. Posting or stating the desired outcome of the meeting helps guide the meeting toward the stated objective.

There is an old saying, "War is the ultimate failure of diplomacy". You only have to look at modern history, in particular events in the Middle East in the past thirty years to see the truth in this statement. Think about those events the next time you decide not to attempt to resolve a conflict in your area of responsibility. In closing this chapter I hope the points I have given you are helpful and once again, just trust the process.

CHAPTER 15

Counseling Employees

As a supervisor one of the most challenging and difficult tasks you have is counseling your employees on performance issues. Issues such as productivity, attendance and violations of work rules, such as insubordination, sleeping on the job and fighting, just to site a few. In approaching a disciplinary type of counseling session I must advise you to always try to use facts and not opinions, when you are trying to make your points with the employee. In other words be objective and not subjective. Also, as I pointed out in Chapter Seven, follow the golden rule of counseling, never counsel an employee alone. Always have a third party present, especially when counseling a member of the opposite sex. But, before I go any farther in this chapter, let me take pause and give you an example of what I am talking about. There is certain information that I will leave out of this story to protect the parties that were involved. However, this example is based on actual facts, and is true.

A few years ago I worked with an assistant principal of a middle school. He had worked in the education system for thirty years. He loved what he did for a living and was well on his way to becoming a principal. Being a principal was his life's ambition. Also, he loved working with young people and found it very rewarding. The staff at the school loved him because he supported them in every way possible. After all, he started his career teaching in the classroom, so he had no trouble relating to what teachers had to deal with on day-to-day basis. He was an outstanding educator and a sterling individual. Sometimes life allows us to get away many times with making a mistake before that mistake turns into a sting that leaves a deep and lasting wound. Such was the case with the gentleman in my story.

At the end of every school day students were lined up at tables in the school cafeteria by school bus number. As the bus with the corresponding number on the table came up to the front door, that bus number was called out and the student started moving forward to board the bus. On the particular day in question two of the students got into a fight during the loading procedure. My friend, the assistant principal led the two warriors to the front office of the school. He then proceeded to take the students into his private office one at a time, closing the door behind him. I am sure he had done this many times in the past. To make a long story short he decided to suspend the boys from school for fighting. When one of the students got home from school he told his parents that the assistant principal had gotten physical with him by throwing him against the wall and choking him. The parents, acting like parents, believed the boy and the next day they contacted the school principal and made a complaint. They also filed charges with the District Attorney's office and retained a lawyer to start a lawsuit. After all, this is America, is this not the way it usually goes. The educator was moved out of his position and placed into a temporary position in the central office of the

Board of Education, until the matter was brought to resolution. But wait, this is the United States, and aren't we innocent until proven guilty in a court of law. However, this rule does not always cover the court of public opinion. Also, there were no witnesses. The educator had an excellent reputation and had never been accused of anything like this before. Why didn't they take his word over the students? Needless to say, the educator said the student to get out of being punished at home fabricated this story. I guess all of this initially worked in the students favor. However, life being what it is good people always come out on top in a story like this one, but not always unscarred.

A general officer that I once worked for in the military, taught me to always protect my reputation and keep it clean. In a situation like the one I have just described it can be the thing that saves your day. The local teachers union assigned an attorney to defend my friend in court. The day of the criminal hearing the student and his family were no shows. The charges were dropped, like they should have ever been filed in the first place by the prosecutor. Eventually, so was the civil suit. So you say end of story and life goes back to normal and today the educator is the principal of a school, doing what he does best. Educating our children. Wrong answer! The subject of this story retired a few months after the dust settled on this situation. After thirty years of working with and educating our children he swore that he would never work with young people again. Even though he was never found guilty of the charges, he knew that he would never achieve his goal of being a principal. I can only imagine the mental and physical stress he must have endured. It did leave a scar. One of the last things I said to him, if only you had brought a third party into the office, or left the office door open so that your secretary could have heard what was going on inside. If he had done this do you think this story would have had a different ending? This example is one of many that I have heard about or experienced during my long management career, concerning not using a third party in counseling sessions, that went sour. Hopefully, this story will once again serve to make my key point on the counseling of employees. Always have a third party present.

Some additional key points in counseling I must make, are document all counseling sessions in writing. Have the employee sign the counseling sheet, as well as any witness in the room. Employees have a convenient tendency of forgetting they were ever in a previous counseling session. If the offense is a serious one that may result in loss of pay or time off, make sure you have discussed the issue with the personnel manager and your supervisor before discussing it with the employee. In most organizations today this is policy. On the next two pages I have provided a sample counseling form that I feel is a good standard for use. Once you have used this form and it is signed, it should be secured in a safe and locked location for the future. If the employee wants a copy of the form give it to them.

Another consideration when counseling employees is always conduct the session in a quiet and private area. If you do not have one in your operational area, find one in another location. Borrow someone's office if necessary. It should be a location that is free of ringing phones and prying eyes. Additionally, give the person that you are counseling your undivided attention. Phones tend to draw on that attention, along with employees barging into the office where the counseling is taking place. Sometimes if your office or counseling area is located in a busy area you might think about hanging a do not disturb sign on the door.

John H. Doe Inc.

23 West Smith Street

Dover, Texas 21171

613-217-8800

Employee Counseling Form *(Sample)*

Date _____

Location _____

Employees Name _____

Subject of Counseling Session _____

Issues Discussed _____

_____

_____

_____

_____

_____

_____

_____

_____

Employee Comments _____

_____

_____

_____

_____

_____

_____

_____

_____

Results of Counseling _____

_____

Employee Signature _____

Supervisor Signature _____ **Witness** _____

When possible always try to convey to the employee that the purpose of the session is to help them improve their work performance, not punish them. For example if they are having a problem getting to work on time start the counseling session by stating that you are there to see what you can do to help them improve. Work to keep the session positive, not negative. I am not so naive that I do not realize that this is just not always possible. Particularly, if this is the third time this month you have had to counsel the employee for the same problem. At such a point you might need to deliver a stronger message than you did in previous sessions. Never get hostile or embarrass an employee in a counseling session, and never lose your temper. If you do the later, you will no longer control the session? Strive to keep an even tone in your voice.

If you are supervising an operation such as police, armed security or military type of operation think about this, never counsel someone while they are armed. People can lose their tempers and when guns are present it is never a good thing. Always protect yourself and your employees. Be safe, not sorry.

Again, one rule that I always set before I start a counseling session is that only one person will talk at a time. Get the employee to agree to this. If this rule starts to get violated, I quick refer back to the rule to bring good order back to the session. You must control the session, not the employee. A favorite tactic that people will use in a counseling is that of trying to switch you from the offense to the defense. For example if the session is about staying too long on the lunch break the employee will say, "Well, I see you come back late from lunch all the time". If this happens do not try to start explaining yourself, just say, we are here to talk about your situation and not mine. Their statement may or may not be true, but you must remember the purpose of the statement is to throw you off balance and put you on the defense. You cannot let this happen.

In summary, as I have stated before, counseling is one of the more difficult tasks that a supervisor faces. But if you follow a few simple rules it can be less challenging. First, never counsel an employee alone. Second, state the rule up front that only one person will talk at a time and get the employee to buy into this rule. Third, use a quiet and private location for the counseling session. Fourth, use facts to counsel, not opinions, when possible. Fifth, never let an employee throw you off balance by putting you on the defensive. Finally, document the session in writing; making sure the employee has signed the counseling form. Be sure you retain that written record in a secure location for the future. I hope all of this is helpful and will make your next employee counseling session a little smoother.

CHAPTER 16

Helping Troubled Employees

The most outstanding employee you have working for you, with the most brilliant performance record, at the vanguard of your organization, can become a troubled employee. Literally overnight. At this point you might be saying to yourself, what does this author mean by a troubled employee. Is that someone that is a constant disciplinary problem? The answer to that question is no. Perhaps I can better articulate what I define as a troubled employee. It is real simple; it is someone that has some kind of personal problem that is affecting his or her job performance. The problem can range from money to medical problems and everything in between. When I worked for the Federal Government they had a program to help troubled employees. For about five years I managed the program for my specific agency. It was an excellent program and helped a huge number of people. With the help of many professionals I trained my counselors to just listen to the employee's problems. Then find them the professional help they needed to solve the problem. But, wait a minute you might say why as a supervisor should I even bother helping a troubled employee. The answer is a simple one, take care of your people and they will take care of you. Remember, loyalty is a two way street. I have had employees that just did an outstanding job at everything they worked on. Then one day you happen to notice that their job performance has suddenly gone downhill and fast. You call them into too your office along with their shift manager; remember what I said about talking to employees alone. During the course of the conversation they breakdown and start crying. They tell you that their spouse has just left them for another person. They say that they are having trouble keeping their mind on their work. When I was going through my divorce a few years ago, I had a Plant Manager tell me to just separate my work from my personal problems. If you ever go through a bad family situation, like a divorce or the death of a spouse, you know they are pretty much one in the same, just try that. Let me know how that works out for you. So how do you help this individual? Let me tell you what you don't do and that is start acting like a marriage counselor. You know why? Because you are just not qualified to take on such a task. In fact, unprofessional advice, given by the untrained, can even take a bad situation and make it dangerous. One of the first things that you do is look at their medical insurance and see if it covers marriage or mental health counseling. Most do! Also, see if the employee is a member of a church. You know the clergy are almost always trained to handle matters that require counseling. Most of them are also very good at it. This is something they do a great deal of in the process of taking care of their congregations.

Sometimes the issue concerns money problems. Many companies have policies where they make small loans or give cash advances on paychecks. They recover the money by taking a small amount every week out of the employee's paycheck. When you do have such a policy make sure you have a good recovery system. When I worked for Maryland Cup Corporation they set up their own Credit Union in their Owing Mills, Maryland plant. All loans were paid by payroll deduction and the lending rates were very low.

What ever the problem is you can find help for the employee by using one of the greatest sources of information we have at hand today, the Internet. As many of you know it is just a matter of using a good search engine, like Google, to assist you in your search for the information you are seeking.

If an employee ever tells you that they are thinking of suicide, get them medical help immediately. Such statements are cries for help and when those cries go unanswered the individual may make a stronger statement by actually taking their life. Believe me you do not want to live with the thought that if they are successful you were responsible. Many municipality have suicide hot lines that you can access immediately just by calling 411 (Directory Assistance). Also, you could even consider taking the employee to the emergency room or company doctor. Always get the approval and involvement of a higher authority before doing this, for example your personnel office or supervisor.

One of the toughest problems that I ever had to handle in my years as a manager and supervisor, concerned an employee that had just found out they had AIDS. Again, I cannot give you the name of individuals involved or whom I was working for at the time the incident occurred. This of course is being done for the protection of everyone that was involved. It occurred at a time when AIDS was just coming to the forefront of the nightly medical news. The general public knew very little about HIV and AIDS, other than it occurred in homosexuals and it was fatal. This individual was scared to death and even talking suicide. Their supervisor and fellow employees wanted the individual removed from the building. They feared contamination. This was a real mess. A great deal of ignorance was at play here. I made a few calls to some medical professionals I knew and managed to get the individual into an AIDS victims support program; the individual was already under a medical doctor's care. I then did some research on AIDS and proceeded to educate employees with safety concerns, in order to arrest their fears. All this took some effort, but is was well worth it. I may have saved a life. Thank goodness medicine and the public know more today about AIDS than we did at the time of this incident.

One of the worst mistakes that you as a leader can make when dealing with a troubled employee is to break the confidence that they have placed in you by sharing their problems with other employees. It is critical that you limit the information they have given you to only people that need to know. Such as your supervisor and perhaps personnel manager. If what you have been told in confidence leaks out, and you are responsible, you could be liable. The second biggest mistake is to give the employee your untrained advice. Listen and then find them help. Leave the advice giving to the professionals.

In closing this chapter let me sum up this subject by saying that I hope my words and experiences will help you have a better understanding of how to help a troubled employee. But in the process of giving this help always think about the legal aspect of getting too involved or trying to act like a minister or doctor. Be a good listener and get them the professional help they need. The sooner the better!

CHAPTER 17

Final Thougths

Once you have finished reading "No Natural Born Leaders" place the book on your desk and for the time being forget it is there. As time goes on use it as a reference. It may help you find the guidance you are looking for to overcome a specific problem or situation. In writing "No Natural Born Leaders" my hope was that you would gain knowledge from my own leadership experience and use it to become a solid leader and manager.

In closing this book I must go back to the reason for writing it in the first place. I was hoping that my years of learning would help change the world one person at a time. I found myself sitting on the sidelines and watching while poor leadership and greed slowly destroyed our society. I found myself tiring of stories depicting the foul way in which some managers and companies are treating their employees. I also believe that if more of our learning institutions were teaching Leadership 101, these very same managers might be more professional and ethical human beings. They would care about the welfare of those they have under their supervision. For all the bad managers that lack leadership skills and read, "No Natural Born Leaders" remember it is not to late in life to change your way of doing business. To the young people just starting their careers, think about what you have just read. Give it time to sink in, and then start using it effectively. Finally, to every one that reads "No Natural Born Leaders" I say that when the final page of your book of life is closed, you will account to a higher authority for your actions in this world. If you have in this life mistreated your employees, making their lives miserable because you lack the skills to lead properly, you will pay a heavy price for your actions in the next life. Burn these final thoughts into your mind and think about them everyday for the rest of your career.